Ultimate Manilow

Piano · Vocal · Guitar

ISBN 978-0-634-05068-8

HAL•LEONARD®
CORPORATION
7777 W. BLUEMOUND RD. P.O. BOX 13819 MILWAUKEE, WI 53213

Visit Hal Leonard Online at
www.halleonard.com

Ultimate Manilow

CONTENTS

MANDY

Words and Music by SCOTT ENGLISH
and RICHARD KERR

BANDSTAND BOOGIE
from the Television Series AMERICAN BANDSTAND

Special Lyric by BARRY MANILOW and BRUCE SUSSMAN
Music by CHARLES ALBERTINE

Band - stand. ____ Band - stand. ____ Band - stand.

What-da-ya know, ____ here on the show read-y to go, ____

____ what_ a pro! Hey!___ I'm mak-in' my mark; Gee, this

joint is jump-in'.___ They made such a ___ fuss ___ just ___ to see us ar-rive.

Hey!__ It's Mis - ter Dick Clark; what a place you've got here,

swell spot, the mu - sic's hot here. Best in the East, give it

at least a sev - en - ty - five! Now for

Band - stand.__

Stroll on A - mer - i - can, Lin - dy Hop and Slop, it's A - mer - i - can

Eb9   D7+5   Db13   C7   Bmaj7

tune in, I'm on, turn on, I'm in, I'm on!

Bb6   Eb9   Eb/F

To - day, _____

C7   Bmaj7   Bb6

Band - stand. __

IT'S A MIRACLE

Lyric by MARTY PANZER
Music by BARRY MANILOW

(who who who)   (who)   (who who who)

Now you're here __ and my arms __ are a - round __ you and ba - by, there'll be

dan - cin' in ____ the streets;   there's gon-na be   dan - cin' in ____ the streets,

woh _____   dan - cin' in ___ the   streets. _____

COULD IT BE MAGIC

Inspired by "Prelude in C Minor" by F. Chopin

Words and Music by BARRY MANILOW
and ADRIENNE ANDERSON

Ba - by, I want__ you.

Could it be mag - ic? 1. Come,
2., 3. Now,
come,
now,

I WRITE THE SONGS

Words and Music by
BRUCE JOHNSTON

TRYIN' TO GET THE FEELING AGAIN

Words and Music by
DAVID POMERANZ

WEEKEND IN NEW ENGLAND

Words and Music by
RANDY EDELMAN

THIS ONE'S FOR YOU

Lyric by MARTY PANZER
Music by BARRY MANILOW

1. This one - 'll nev - er sell, __ they'll nev - er un - der - stand, __
2. I've done a hun - dred songs, __ from fan - ta - sies __ to lies, __
I've got it all, __ it seems, __ for all it means __ to me, __

I don't e - ven sing __ it well, __ I try, but I __ just can't. __ But I
But this one's so real __ for me __ that I'm the one __ who cries. __ But I
But I sing of things __ I miss __ and things that used __ to be. __ And I

LOOKS LIKE WE MADE IT

Words and Music by RICHARD KERR
and WILL JENNINGS

There you are,_____ look-in' just the same as you did last time I
Love's so strange,_ play-ing hide and seek with hearts and al - ways

touched you. And here I am,___ close to get-tin' tan-gled up___ in - side the
hurt - ing. And we're the fools,_ stand-ing close e - nough to touch_ those burn-ing

thought of you. Do you love him as much as I___ love her? And will that love be
mem - o - ries. And if I hold you for the sake of all___ those times love made us lose our

DAYBREAK

Words and Music by BARRY MANILOW
and ADRIENNE ANDERSON

1. Sing-in' to the world, it's time we let the spir-it come in,
2. Sing-in' to the world, what's the point in put-tin' it down,

— Let it come on in, I'm sing-in' to the world, ev-
— There's so much love to share, I'm sing-in' to the world, don't

— ry-bod-y's caught in the spin, We've been
— you see it all comes a-round, The feel-ing's ev-'ry-where, We've been

CAN'T SMILE WITHOUT YOU

Words and Music by CHRIS ARNOLD,
DAVID MARTIN and GEOFF MORROW

EVEN NOW

Lyric by MARTY PANZER
Music by BARRY MANILOW

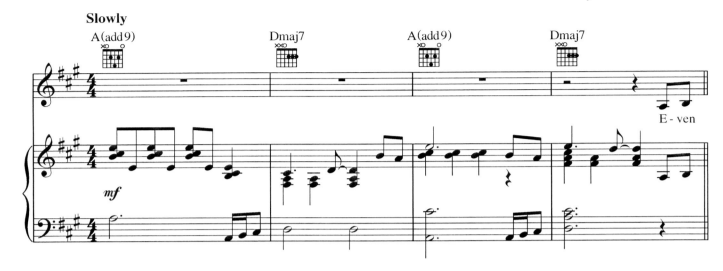

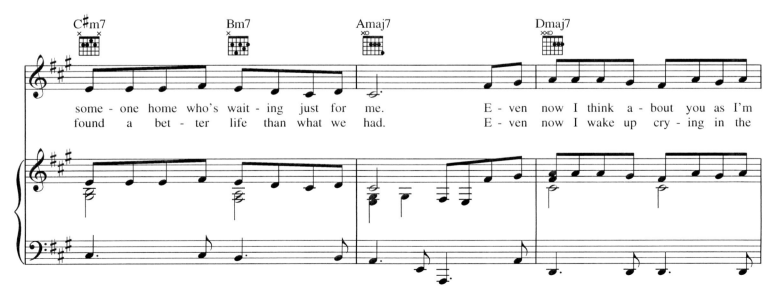

COPACABANA
(At the Copa)

Music by BARRY MANILOW
Lyric by BRUCE SUSSMAN and JACK FELDMAN

Moderately, with a Latin feel

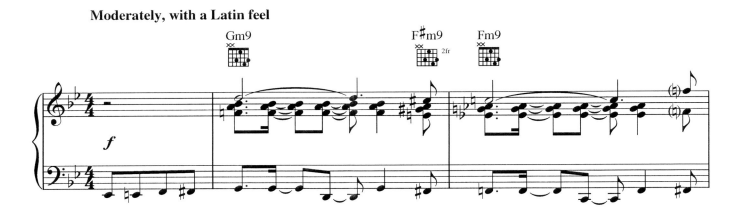

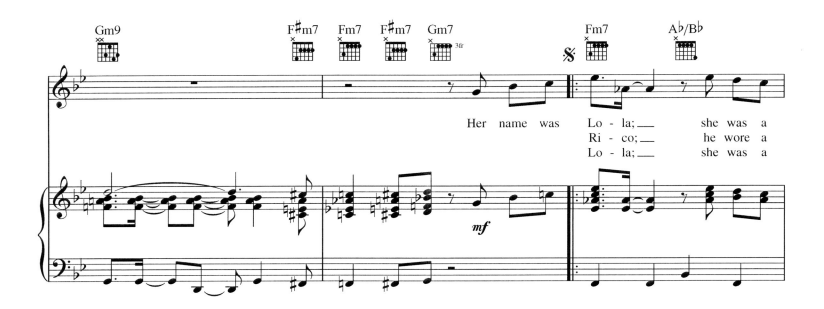

Her name was Lo - la;___ she was a
Ri - co;___ he wore a
Lo - la;___ she was a

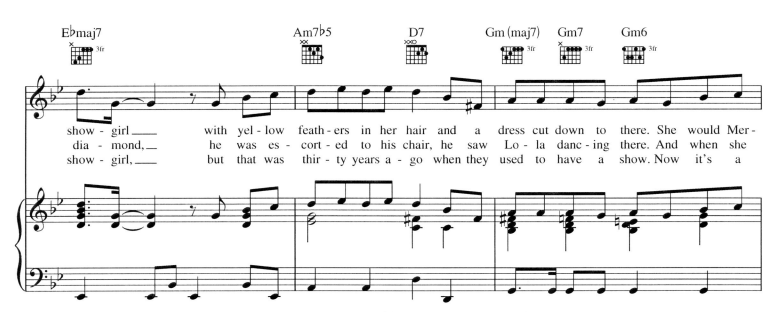

show - girl___ with yel - low feath - ers in her hair and a dress cut down to there. She would Mer -
dia - mond,___ he was es - cort - ed to his chair, he saw Lo - la danc - ing there. And when she
show - girl,___ but that was thir - ty years a - go when they used to have a show. Now it's a

ban - a, _____ like in __ Ha - van - a, _____

__ have a __ ba - nan - a, _____ mu - sic __ and

pas - sion _____ al - ways __ in fash - ion.

Instrumental solo ad lib.

SOMEWHERE IN THE NIGHT

Words and Music by WILL JENNINGS
and RICHARD KERR

READY TO TAKE A CHANCE AGAIN
(Love Theme)
from the Paramount Picture FOUL PLAY

Words by NORMAN GIMBEL
Music by CHARLES FOX

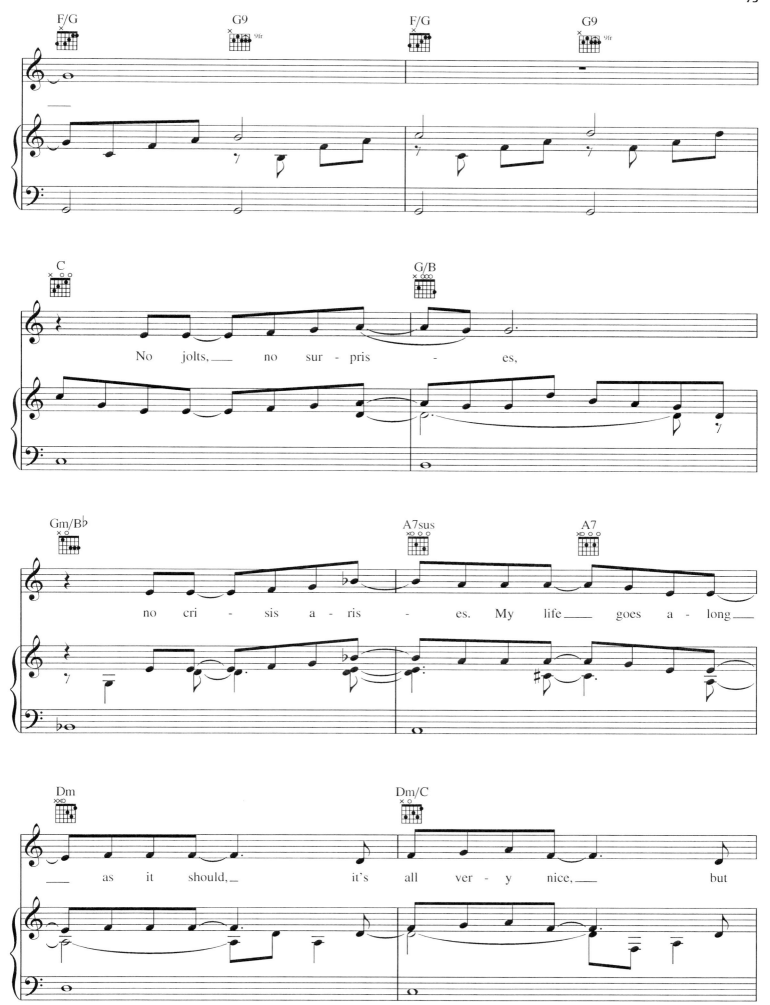

No jolts,___ no sur - pris - - es,

no cri - sis a - ris - - es. My life___ goes a - long___

___ as it should,___ it's all ver - y nice,___ but

I MADE IT THROUGH THE RAIN

Words and Music by BARRY MANILOW, JACK FELDMAN,
BRUCE SUSSMAN, DREY SHEPPERD and GERARD KENNY

SHIPS

Words and Music by
IAN HUNTER

THE OLD SONGS

Words and Music by BUDDY KAYE
and DAVID POMERANZ

WHEN OCTOBER GOES

Words by JOHNNY MERCER
Music by BARRY MANILOW

SOMEWHERE DOWN THE ROAD

Words and Music by CYNTHIA WEIL
and TOM SNOW

Slowly

We had the right love at the wrong time.
Some-times good-byes are not for-ev-er; It

guess I al-ways knew in-side I would-n't have you for a long
does-n't mat-ter if you're gone, I still be-lieve in us to-geth-

time. Those dreams of yours are shin-in' on
-er. I un-der-stand more than you